# Francis Frith's
# AROUND PLYMOUTH

PHOTOGRAPHIC MEMORIES

# Francis Frith's
# AROUND PLYMOUTH

◆

Martin Dunning

FRITH
BOOK Co

First published in the United Kingdom in 2000 by
Frith Book Company Ltd

Hardback Edition 2000
ISBN 1-85937-119-1

Paperback Edition 2001
ISBN 1-85937-389-5

Reprinted in Hardback 2001
ISBN 1-85937-119-1

British Library Cataloguing in Publication Data

Francis Frith's Around Plymouth
Martin Dunning

Frith Book Company Ltd
Frith's Barn, Teffont,
Salisbury, Wiltshire SP3 5QP
Tel: +44 (0) 1722 716 376
Email: info@francisfrith.co.uk
www.francisfrith.co.uk


Printed and bound in Great Britain

# Contents

# FRANCIS FRITH: *Victorian Pioneer*

**FRANCIS FRITH**, Victorian founder of the world-famous photographic archive, was a complex and multitudinous man. A devout Quaker and a highly successful Victorian businessman, he was both philosophic by nature and pioneering in outlook.

By 1855 Francis Frith had already established a wholesale grocery business in Liverpool, and sold it for the astonishing sum of £200,000, which is the equivalent today of over £15,000,000. Now a multi-millionaire, he was able to indulge his passion for travel. As a child he had pored over travel books written by early explorers, and his fancy and imagination had been stirred by family holidays to the sublime mountain regions of Wales and Scotland. 'What a land of spirit-stirring and enriching scenes and places!' he had written. He was to return to these scenes of grandeur in later years to 'recapture the thousands of vivid and tender memories', but with a different purpose. Now in his thirties, and captivated by the new science of photography, Frith set out on a series of pioneering journeys to the Nile regions that occupied him from 1856 until 1860.

## INTRIGUE AND ADVENTURE

He took with him on his travels a specially-designed wicker carriage that acted as both dark-room and sleeping chamber. These far-flung journeys were packed with intrigue and adventure. In his life story, written when he was sixty-three, Frith tells of being held captive by bandits, and of fighting 'an awful midnight battle to the very point of surrender with a deadly pack of hungry, wild dogs'. Sporting flowing Arab costume, Frith arrived at Akaba by camel seventy years before Lawrence, where he encountered 'desert princes and rival sheikhs, blazing with jewel-hilted swords'.

During these extraordinary adventures he was assiduously exploring the desert regions bordering the Nile and patiently recording the antiquities and peoples with his camera. He was the first photographer to venture beyond the sixth cataract. Africa was still the mysterious 'Dark Continent', and Stanley and Livingstone's historic meeting was a decade into the future. The conditions for picture taking confound belief. He laboured for hours in his wicker dark-room in the sweltering heat of the desert, while the volatile chemicals fizzed dangerously in their trays. Often he was forced to work in remote tombs and caves where conditions were cooler. Back in London he exhibited his photographs and was 'rapturously cheered' by members of the Royal Society. His reputation as a photographer was made overnight. An eminent modern historian has likened their impact on the population of the time to that on our own generation of the first photographs taken on the surface of the moon.

## VENTURE OF A LIFE-TIME

Characteristically, Frith quickly spotted the opportunity to create a new business as a specialist publisher of photographs. He lived in an era of immense and sometimes violent change. For the poor in the early part of Victoria's reign work was a drudge and the hours long, and people had precious little free time to enjoy themselves.

Most had no transport other than a cart or gig at their disposal, and had not travelled far beyond the boundaries of their own town or village. However, by the 1870s, the railways had threaded their way across the country, and Bank Holidays and half-day Saturdays had been made obligatory by Act of Parliament. All of a sudden the ordinary working man and his family were able to enjoy days out and see a little more of the world.

With characteristic business acumen, Francis Frith foresaw that these new tourists would enjoy having souvenirs to commemorate their days out. In 1860 he married Mary Ann Rosling and set out with the intention of photographing every city, town and village in Britain. For the next thirty years he travelled the country by train and by pony and trap, producing fine photographs of seaside resorts and beauty spots that were keenly bought by millions of Victorians. These prints were painstakingly pasted into family albums and pored over during the dark nights of winter, rekindling precious memories of summer excursions.

## THE RISE OF FRITH & CO

Frith's studio was soon supplying retail shops all over the country. To meet the demand he gathered about him a small team of photographers, and published the work of independent artist-photographers of the calibre of Roger Fenton and Francis Bedford. In order to gain some understanding of the scale of Frith's business one only has to look at the catalogue issued by Frith & Co in 1886: it runs to some 670

pages, listing not only many thousands of views of the British Isles but also many photographs of most European countries, and China, Japan, the USA and Canada – note the sample page shown above from the hand-written *Frith & Co* ledgers detailing pictures taken. By 1890 Frith had created the greatest specialist photographic publishing company in the world, with over 2,000 outlets – more than the combined number that Boots and WH Smith have today! The picture on the right shows the *Frith & Co* display board at Ingleton in the Yorkshire Dales. Beautifully constructed with mahogany frame and gilt inserts, it could display up to a dozen local scenes.

## POSTCARD BONANZA

The ever-popular holiday postcard we know today took many years to develop. In 1870 the Post Office issued the first plain cards, with a pre-printed stamp on one face. In 1894 they allowed other publishers' cards to be sent through the mail with an attached adhesive halfpenny stamp. Demand grew rapidly, and in 1895 a new size of postcard was permitted called the

court card, but there was little room for illustration. In 1899, a year after Frith's death, a new card measuring 5.5 x 3.5 inches became the standard format, but it was not until 1902 that the divided back came into being, with address and message on one face and a full-size illustration on the other. *Frith & Co* were in the vanguard of postcard development, and Frith's sons Eustace and Cyril continued their father's monumental task, expanding the number of views offered to the public and recording more and more places in Britain, as the coasts and countryside were opened up to mass travel.

Francis Frith died in 1898 at his villa in Cannes, his great project still growing. The archive he created continued in business for another seventy years. By 1970 it contained over a third of a million pictures of 7,000 cities, towns and villages. The massive photographic record Frith has left to us stands as a living monument to a special and very remarkable man.

# Frith's Archive: *A Unique Legacy*

**FRANCIS FRITH'S** legacy to us today is of immense significance and value, for the magnificent archive of evocative photographs he created provides a unique record of change in 7,000 cities, towns and villages throughout Britain over a century and more. Frith and his fellow studio photographers revisited locations many times down the years to update their views, compiling for us an enthralling and colourful pageant of British life and character.

We tend to think of Frith's sepia views of Britain as nostalgic, for most of us use them to conjure up memories of places in our own lives with which we have family associations. It often makes us forget that to Francis Frith they were records of daily life as it was actually being lived in the cities, towns and villages of his day. The Victorian age was one of great and often bewildering change for ordinary people, and though the pictures evoke an impression of slower times, life was as busy and hectic as it is today.

We are fortunate that Frith was a photographer of the people, dedicated to recording the minutiae of everyday life. For it is this sheer wealth of visual data, the painstaking chronicle of changes in dress, transport, street layouts, buildings, housing, engineering and landscape that captivates us so much today. His remarkable images offer us a powerful link with the past and with the lives of our ancestors.

## TODAY'S TECHNOLOGY

Computers have now made it possible for Frith's many thousands of images to be accessed almost instantly. In the Frith archive today, each photograph is carefully 'digitised' then stored on a CD Rom. Frith archivists can locate a single photograph amongst thousands within seconds. Views can be catalogued and sorted under a variety of categories of place and content to the immediate benefit of researchers. Inexpensive reference prints can be created for them at the touch of a mouse button, and a wide range of books and other printed materials assembled and published for a wider, more general readership - in the next twelve months over a hundred Frith local history titles will be published! The

**See Frith at www.francisfrith.co.uk**

10

day-to-day workings of the archive are very different from how they were in Francis Frith's time: imagine the herculean task of sorting through eleven tons of glass negatives as Frith had to do to locate a particular sequence of pictures! Yet the archive still prides itself on maintaining the same high standards of excellence laid down by Francis Frith, including the painstaking cataloguing and indexing of every view.

It is curious to reflect on how the internet now allows researchers in America and elsewhere greater instant access to the archive than Frith himself ever enjoyed. Many thousands of individual views can be called up on screen within seconds on one of the Frith internet sites, enabling people living continents away to revisit the streets of their ancestral home town, or view places in Britain where they have enjoyed holidays. Many overseas researchers welcome the chance to view special theme selections, such as transport, sports, costume and ancient monuments.

We are certain that Francis Frith would have heartily approved of these modern developments, for he himself was always working at the very limits of Victorian photographic technology.

## THE VALUE OF THE ARCHIVE TODAY

Because of the benefits brought by the computer, Frith's images are increasingly studied by social historians, by researchers into genealogy and ancestory, by architects, town planners, and by teachers and schoolchildren involved in local history projects. In addition, the archive offers every one of us a unique opportunity to examine the places where we and our families have lived and worked down the years. Immensely successful in Frith's own era, the archive is now, a century and more on, entering a new phase of popularity.

## THE PAST IN TUNE WITH THE FUTURE

Historians consider the Francis Frith Collection to be of prime national importance. It is the only archive of its kind remaining in private ownership and has been valued at a million pounds. However, this figure is now rapidly increasing as digital technology enables more and more people around the world to enjoy its benefits.

Francis Frith's archive is now housed in an historic timber barn in the beautiful village of Teffont in Wiltshire. Its founder would not recognize the archive office as it is today. In place of the many thousands of dusty boxes containing glass plate negatives and an all-pervading odour of photographic chemicals, there are now ranks of computer screens. He would be amazed to watch his images travelling round the world at unimaginable speeds through network and internet lines.

The archive's future is both bright and exciting. Francis Frith, with his unshakeable belief in making photographs available to the greatest number of people, would undoubtedly approve of what is being done today with his lifetime's work. His photographs, depicting our shared past, are now bringing pleasure and enlightenment to millions around the world a century and more after his death.

# AROUND PLYMOUTH – *An Introduction*

DESPITE THE ROLE it has played in many of Britain's great historic moments and periods, Plymouth is a city apart. Although only 200 miles from London - the same distance as, say, Manchester or Liverpool - its location on the far south-west peninsula has given Plymouth an isolation, even today, that other great cities lack. And it is not merely distance that has isolated the city - its site is bounded on all sides by obstacles. To the north are the stern hills of Dartmoor, to the east the River Plym and to the west the Tamar. Early visitors to the peninsula on which the city would eventually grow would have had to wait for the tide at the Ebb Ford, where Marsh Mills roundabout now stands, before they could cross the Plym and put their feet up at the Crabtree Inn, which over the centuries welcomed many a tired and mud-spattered traveller. Those coming from the west had two choices: to travel north to Gunnislake, the lowest bridge on the Tamar and some twenty miles up the river, and thence via Tavistock and Roborough Down, or to take the ferry that ran at Saltash across the strong tides of the Tamar. Even for land travellers, Plymouth was a place governed by the tides.

Plymouth grew from several small settlements, one of the earliest being Mountbatten, at the mouth of the Plym. The site of an Iron Age cemetery, Mountbatten is thought to have been a trading post from as early as 1000 BC, and in Roman times exported cattle, hides and tin - the first indication of the maritime future of the area. Opposite Mountbatten the small fishing village of Sutton grew around the sheltered harbour of Sutton Pool; it eventually became a town when it was granted a market in 1254 by Henry III. By this time, ships loading tin from the rich port of Plympton had started to use Sutton too, and a lively trade was developing. Fish, hides, lead, wool and cloth were exported, while iron, fruit, wine, onions, garlic and wheat were landed.

1295 saw an event that was to point the way for future development when Edward I assembled the fleet at Plymouth for the first time. The port occupies a crucial strategic position guarding the Western Approaches; it was this factor that was to cement Plymouth's importance, and was probably a consideration when Henry VI granted the borough charter in 1439.

If Plymouth's maritime status brought prosperity, it also meant that the port was often in the front line, especially when Spain was involved. Francis Drake, knighted by Elizabeth I for his circumnavigation of the globe in 1577-80, sailed from Plymouth to 'singe the King of Spain's beard' at Cadiz in 1587 and returned to face his sternest test in 1588 - the Spanish Armada. His apparent bravado on insisting that he finish his game of bowls before engaging the mighty Spanish fleet was dictated by the mundane fact that his ships could not sail until the tide had turned, but what is not in doubt is that his courage and seamanship helped carry the day for the English fleet. Drake did not, as is commonly believed, command the fleet - that responsibility fell to Lord Howard.

Years of fighting Catholic Spain probably explain the streak of puritanism that Plymouth showed for the next hundred years. The city welcomed the noncomformist Pilgrim Fathers when the Mayflower put in for repairs and provisions before sailing for the New World in 1620, and during the Civil War it took Cromwell's side. Plymouth was isolated, as Barnstaple, Bideford and Exeter were all captured by the Royalists and Royalist ships blockaded the Sound.

The nine thousand Parliamentarian troops garrisoned at Plymouth held out under siege for two years, winning a famous victory in December 1643 in the battle which raged around Tothill and Freedom Park. Prince Maurice Road and Mount Gould are named after the Royalist and Parliamentarian commanders. Plymouth was eventually relieved in March 1645 when Cromwell and Fairfax met in the city.

Upon the Restoration of the Monarchy, Charles II decided that Plymouth's defences needed strengthening and commissioned the building of the Citadel. One of the finest and largest restoration forts in the country, it boasted upon completion 152 guns, some of which faced the city as a reminder to

Plymothians of their true place in the order of things.

Secretary of the Navy Samuel Pepys, now known for his diaries but also effectively the founder of the Royal Navy as we know it, visited Plymouth with Charles in 1676 to inspect sites for a new Royal Dockyard. Turnchapel, at the mouth of the Plym, was considered, but struggled for the first half of the 18th century. Fishing still thrived, particularly for pilchards, and trade carried on, but Plymouth has never figured near the top of the table as a commercial port because of its isolation and the lack of nearby markets. Bristol and Liverpool made fortunes from the slave trade, and London's demand for commodities ensured

eventually the prize was given to the Tamar. The Tamar's disadvantages - strong tides, a narrow and winding entrance and often contrary winds - also acted in its favour as they gave the river natural defences from attack; work started on what is now Devonport's South Yard in 1691. Another sign of the port's growing stature was the building in 1696 of Winstanley's 120-foot lighthouse on the Eddystone Rocks fourteen miles off the Hoe, the first in a series of four that would culminate in the current lighthouse built by Douglas in 1878.

Investment notwithstanding, Plymouth that her docks were always busy, but Plymouth slumbered on, depressed and waiting for a turn in the tides of history.

War, by now a recurring theme in the fortunes of the city, provided the catalyst. From 1756 a succession of conflicts - the Seven Years' War, the American War of Independence and the Napoleonic Wars - caused an upturn in Plymouth's fortunes. Her isolation was eased in 1758 with the completion of the Great West Road, although it still took twelve hours to reach Exeter. The Royal Naval Hospital in Stonehouse was built in 1758-62, the dockyard bustled, and in 1812 the famous Scots engineer John Rennie began the construction of the Breakwater. A massive undertaking which was not completed until 1841, the Breakwater was a crucial development. Generations of mariners such as Grenville, Howard and Raleigh had complained that the relatively narrow entrances to the Plym and Tamar were dangerous in foul weather; mariners would often run before the storm to anchor in the sheltered waters of Tor Bay. Now, all a gale-battered ship had to do was slip in through the eastern or western entrances and move into the lee of the breakwater, with plenty of sea-room and calm water in which to anchor.

The railways arrived in 1848-9, and at last Plymouth had a rapid connection with the rest of the country. Isambard Kingdom Brunel's magnificent railway bridge over the Tamar, completed shortly before the great man's death in 1859, had more than a mere practical significance - it was a symbol of Plymouth moving with the times.

John Foulston's Theatre Royal provided entertainment for those who could afford it, while those of lesser means could promenade on the pier or take the air on the Hoe. In the 1920s and 1930s, transatlantic liners anchored in the Sound, discharging passengers such as Charlie Chaplin, Mary Pickford and Rudolph Valentino to catch their train for London from Millbay Docks.

Plymouth prospered, but the clouds of war were gathering again; during the Second World War the city lived through its darkest hours. As a major naval port, Plymouth was high on the Luftwaffe's target list. A series of intense air raids in 1941 left the city devastated; much of the city centre was reduced to rubble, and fine buildings such as the Theatre Royal, the Royal Hotel, the Post Office and the Municipal Buildings were lost for ever. But the people of Plymouth were unbowed. Thousands left the city each night for the foothills of Dartmoor and safety from the bombs, and returned to work the next day. The shell of St Andrew's Church was planted with flowers and hundreds came to worship in the 'Garden Church', while on hot summer evenings, thousands would come from the ruined city to dance on the Hoe with dignitaries like Lady Nancy Astor MP and cock a defiant snook at Nazism.

Once the war was over, thoughts turned to reconstruction. It is a local joke that what Hitler started, the town planners finished: it is true that the new, geometric street plan of the city centre is a little uninspiring, but St Andrew's still stands, and the broad sweep of Armada Way leads one seawards to the heights of the Hoe.

Stand on the Promenade on a clear day and turn through 360°, and all around are reminders of Plymouth's past. To the north are the blue hills of Dartmoor, source of the tin that caused the port to come into existence. West is the entrance to the Tamar, home to the frigates, aircraft carriers and submarines which slip in and out of port in all weathers, even in peacetime. Merchantmen anchor in the lee of the Breakwater, ready to discharge their cargoes of petrol and fertiliser on the wharves of the Plym, and trawlers set sail from a largely unchanged Barbican for the fishing grounds. And on the horizon, the Eddystone light winks unceasingly, a beacon for mariners heading for one of Britain's great ports.

**THE HOE 1890** 22471

Taken from Devil's Point looking across Firestone bay with the Hoe just visible on the far right. The large colon-naded building is the Winter Villa, built by the Earl of Mount Edgecumbe for his wife, who found the winters at Mount Edgecumbe House a little too draughty.

**VIEW FROM THE HOE c1876** 8349

Taken from the site of the old Hoe Police Station and lock-up before the pier was built, this view shows a largely undeveloped West Hoe (the grassy area at centre). The large block of houses on the point at centre left still stands and is now mostly hotels.

**THE ESPLANADE AND HOE 1889** 22363
One hundred feet above sea level, and with commanding views of the Sound and the English Channel, the Hoe is where Sir Francis Drake is reputed to have played his famous game of bowls while waiting for the Armada to arrive in 1588.

**THE HOE AND PIER 1889** 22368
The prominent structure on the top of Staddon Heights (just right of centre) is not, as local myth says, a windbreak for the golf course on the top of the Heights; it was actually constructed as a gunnery range for troops stationed at Bovisand Fort, on the headland below.

**THE ESPLANADE HOE 1889** 22361
The fine colonnaded building second from left is the
Grand Hotel; it still stands, as does Eliot Terrace to its right.
3 Eliot Terrace was the home of Lord and Lady Astor for
many years. Nancy Astor was the first woman MP in the
country, representing Plymouth Sutton from 1919–46.

**THE PIER FROM SMEATON TOWER 1889** 22372

In the middle distance to the right are ships anchored in the Hamoaze, which turns north up the Tamar to Devonport Dockyard. The narrow entrance to the Hamoaze (hidden at centre) is easily guarded but, in times of sail, presented difficulties for the fleet if it needed to sail in a hurry and on a foul tide.

**THE PIER FROM BELOW 1889** 22375

The building next to the Grand Hotel, a victim of the Luftwaffe in the blitz, became the home of the Royal Western Yacht Club in 1880. The club subsequently moved to West Hoe and, in the 1980s, to Queen Anne's Battery. The doors above the steps on the right were for many years used by the Leander Swimming Club.

**SMEATON TOWER 1890** 22365

This lighthouse once occupied the feared Eddystone Rock, 14 miles south of the Hoe. Built by John Smeaton, it was the third lighthouse on the rock; it shone from 1756 to 1890, when the present lighthouse, designed by Douglas, was completed.

**MOUNT EDGECUMBE 1889** 22385

The wooded estate of Mount Edgecumbe is the hereditary seat of the Earls of Mount Edgecumbe. The clearing in the centre is the site of the famous folly, while on the right the top of Mount Edgecumbe House can be seen peeping from the trees.

**THE PIER 1889** 22377

Plymouth's pier was destroyed in the blitz  It was built in 1884, extending out from the old Bull Ring, a popular spot for political meetings, particularly in the last century during the noisy campaign that led in 1832 to Plymouth becoming three constituencies and Stonehouse and Devonport having their own MPs for the first time.

**THE HOE AND PIER 1890** 27530

The centre of the Pier, now covered, was a popular venue for concert parties, boxing, wrestling, roller skating and tea dances. To take the sea air in the company of other fashionable Victorians, one entered through the turnstiles on each side of the clock for the princely sum of 2d.

**VIEW FROM THE PIER 1892** 30590

The building high up on the left houses the Plymouth Laboratory of the Marine Biological Association of Great Britain, now one of the world's leading marine research organisations. The building also housed the aquarium before the opening of the national marine aquarium on the Barbican in 1998. Right of the MBA is the Citadel, the city's biggest fortress.

**THE PIER 1892**
The steps and diving board below the Sunlight Soap advertisement belonged to the Plymouth Ladies Swimming Club. One ex-member recalls completing the two-mile swim from the Breakwater in 1927 in 58 minutes and two thirds of a second. Her sister held the record of 48 minutes.

**VIEW FROM THE PIER 1892**
The rocks in the centre are where Tinside Pool now stands. Further back, to the right of the triangular buttress, is the site of the Royal Plymouth Corinthian Yacht Club and beyond that, the Cattewater.

**THE PIER 1892** 30585

**VIEW FROM THE PIER 1892** 30591

**THE PIER AND DRAKE'S ISLAND 1892** 30583
Drake's Island was originally known as St Nicholas Island; it was owned by the Priors of Plympton, who used it as a rabbit warren. It was fortified in 1549 and the defences were later extended by Plymouth's favourite son - hence the name change.

**VIEW FROM STADDON 1889** 22383
The Mountbatten peninsula (foreground) guards and shelters the Cattewater and Sutton Pool (right). Occupied since prehistoric times, ownership was returned to the city in 1995 after nearly 70 years of occupation by the RAF. In the 1920s the personnel list included one Aircraftman Shaw - Lawrence of Arabia.

**THE PIER 1898** 41930
The five square miles of Plymouth Sound provide a
fine safe anchorage. Jennycliff Bay (in the middle distance on the left) is as popular a spot now as in 1898,
especially if the wind is in the east and the great bulk
of Staddon Heights acts as a natural windbreak.

**VIEW FROM SMEATON POINT 1898** 41929

The curious octagonal building in the foreground was once the Hoe Police Station and was also a camera obscura. The building by the little harbour was for many years the home of the Royal Western Yacht Club and is now the Waterfront Restaurant.

**THE BREAKWATER 1893** 31954

The completion of the Breakwater in 1844 after 32 years' work secured Plymouth's standing as a major port. Designed by John Rennie, and utilising 3,500,000 tons of limestone from quarries at Oreston, its construction meant that for the first time ships did not have to use the Plym or the Tamar to anchor in a storm.

**THE HOE 1902** 48781

The Bandstand (foreground) once stood on the site of today's public bowling green before moving to this site near Smeaton's Tower. Regular performers included the Royal Marine Band; the Bandstand was hit during the blitz and subsequently pulled down.

**THE PIER 1898** 41931

The paddle steamers ran trips to the River Yealm and as far west as Looe. In a curious echo of history, many of today's tourist boats leave from the site of the old pier for similar destinations, and also for cruises up the Tamar.

**THE HOE 1904** 52403
The area covered by trees below the octagonal Police Station
was for a long time home to the Mallard Café; it is now the
site of the Dome, one of Plymouth's major attractions.

**THE HOE 1904** 52398
The prominent building in the centre was used for many years as a nursery by the city parks department. The exposed position of the bandstand meant that it had to have a revolving glass screen to prevent the performers' music blowing away!

**THE BANDSTAND 1902** 48782
In the middle distance on the left are the masts of ships in Millbay Docks. In the 1920s Millbay Docks were busy with passengers being ferried from the railway out to liners such as the Queen Mary and Normandie.

**THE PIER 1913** 65981

Modern excursion boats are diesel rather than steam, and have propellers instead of paddle wheels. Paddlers lasted longer than is generally known, however: the dockyard was using paddle tugs until the mid 1980s.

**THE HOE, SMEATON TOWER AND BANDSTAND 1913** 65980

The stone pavilion on the left, known to Plymothians as the 'Wedding Cake', was built in 1891-2 when Alderman Harris was Mayor. The garden directly below it is now a garden of remembrance to the dead of Dunkirk, Normandy, Korea, Malaysia and other campaigns.

**SMEATON'S TOWER AND THE BANDSTAND 1913** 65979
As well as being used for promenading, the Hoe has
always been the vantage point from which Plymothians
have watched the arrivals and departures of vessels,
from Sir Francis Chichester's 'Gypsy Moth IV' to the
battle-weary ships of the Falklands war.

**THE PIER 1924** 75896
The Pier not only acted as a magnet for tourists but
also for local traders, who would set up their carts,
wagons and stalls near the entrance hoping to catch
some trade from alighting tram passengers.

**THE PIER AND DRAKE'S ISLAND 1924** 75899

On his return from his circumnavigation in 1580, Drake anchored in the lee of the island while he sent messengers ashore to check if Queen Elizabeth was still alive and, if so, whether he was still in favour. He managed to ensure the latter by sending several tons of stolen Spanish gold to London.

**THE NAVAL AND ARMADA MEMORIALS 1924** 75908

In 1888 the Hoe became a park and the Armada Memorial (left) was erected to mark the tercentenary of Drake's great victory. The Naval Memorial was extended considerably after World War Two.

**THE LIDO AND WALKS 1934** 86216

The magnificent art deco Tinside Lido and Swimming Pool, completed in 1933, was a popular venue for generations of Plymouth children, mainly during the summer holidays, as the salt-water pool had no heating. More sedentary pleasures could be had by hiring a chalet, the roofs of some of which can be seen in the left foreground.

**DRAKE'S STATUE 1930** 83293

The Café on the left was one of Hitler's victims; it was replaced by a vast Nissen Hut, which served teas well into the 1980s. Visible just behind Drake's Statue is the corner of the bowling green. The terrace behind is also gone; the Register Office now stands on the site.

**FROM THE CITADEL 1904** 52400

On the far right, the building with the conservatory and tower is the old Hoegate School. The fine avenue of elm trees on the left suffered greatly from the ravages of Dutch Elm Disease in the 1970s.

**THE ROYAL CITADEL GATE 1924** 75921

Construction of the Citadel commenced in 1670 on the orders of Charles II. It is now home to 29 Commando Regiment Royal Artillery; it was considerably extended in the 1980s. Just visible through the gate are some of the magnificent Restoration buildings that surround the parade ground.

**THE SOUTH AFRICAN MEMORIAL 1904** 52404

Only a year old when this picture was taken, this pink granite obelisk was erected in memory of Christian Victor, Prince of Schleswig Holstein and grandson of Queen Victoria, who died in the Boer War. It also serves as a memorial to the men of the Gloucestershire, Somerset and Devonshire regiments who died in the same campaign. A chip on the south west corner is shrapnel damage from the blitz.

**THE SOUTH AFRICAN MONUMENT AND GUILDHALL 1904** 52399
This view shows the commanding field of fire available to gunners on the Citadel, from where this picture was taken. Plymouth was staunchly parliamentarian during the Civil War; when Charles II built the Citadel, the fact that there were gun emplacements facing inland would not have gone unnoticed by the local population.

**THE BARBICAN 1890** 22474
Built around Sutton Pool, site of one of the original settlements in the area, the Barbican is home to Plymouth's fishing fleet. The cobbled streets and granite steps remain unchanged, but in place of shipping offices and fish salesmen are now ice cream parlours, cafés and souvenir shops.

**SUTTON POOL 1904** 52413A

Declining stocks and fish quotas have taken their toll of the fleet, and Sutton Pool now has far fewer boats. The building on the right is the old Barbican Police Station, now used by Cap'n Jasper's burger bar, and the quay has been extended slightly so that the mooring bollards now sprout from the pavement!

**ONION SELLERS 1907** 59208

The onions on the shoulders of these two boys, photographed at the Mayflower Steps, may well have been French. Breton onion sellers were once a common sight on the streets of Plymouth.

**THE BARBICAN c1955** P60050
The open building on the left, now occupied by Dartington Glass, was until the 1990s the old fish market, built in 1892. The warehouses in the background have been converted into flats, and the area of Sutton Pool on the far right is now a marina.

**THE BARBICAN c1955** P60069
The white painted steps, centre left, are the Mayflower Steps, scene of the Pilgrim Fathers' departure for the New World in 1620. On the right, the coal wharf is now home to the new fish market and National Marine Aquarium, and the harbour now has lock gates to prevent it drying out at low tide.

**ST ANDREW'S CHURCH 1889** 22399

St Andrew's is the mother church of Plymouth; there is evidence that a Christian community used the site as early as the 8th century. Construction of the present building commenced in 1370. The church was burned down in the blitz, but restoration started in 1949 and the church was finally reconsecrated in 1957.

**ST ANDREW'S CROSS 1900** 45862

After St Andrew's had been reduced to a shell by the Luftwaffe in 1941, somebody put a wooden board above the door with the word Resurgam on it, from the Latin for 'I will rise again'. Ever since then the north door (left) of St Andrew's has been known as the Resurgam door.

**THE GUILDHALL 1889** 22394

The fine tower at the west end of St Andrew's, built by Thomas Yogge in 1481 and now housing a peal of ten bells, used to look out over Guildhall Square, which is now a car park.

**THE GUILDHALL AND POST OFFICE 1889** 22388

The Guildhall (left) and Municipal Buildings (right, containing the Lord Mayor's Parlour) were opened in 1874 by the Prince of Wales, who later became Edward VII. They were both gutted by fire on the night of 3 March 1941.

**ST ANDREW'S CROSS 1895** 36320
Erected in 1895 as a memorial after the removal of an ancient burial ground, St Andrew's Cross was damaged the night before the church went up in flames and was subsequently removed. The only remaining piece is the copper cross from the very top, which is now in the north aisle of St Andrew's.

**THE GUILDHALL 1889** 22395
Taken from the vicinity of the Boer War memorial, this picture shows how much more ornate the Guildhall was before its destruction and subsequent rebuilding. The spire on the ridge of the main roof no longer exists, and the tower now has a plain copper roof.

**THE GUILDHALL AND POST OFFICE 1904** 52408
The main public entrance to the Post Office is just out of sight around the corner on the right. Staff entered through the central doors. Telegraphy equipment was housed on the first floor, and the top floor contained the staff rest-rooms.

THE GUILDHALL 1924  75920
The new stained glass window in the tower of St Andrew's, installed after the war, was designed by John Piper (who also designed the windows in the east end); it commemorates Nancy Astor and her husband, who were Mayor and Mayoress during the war years.

OLD TOWN STREET 1889  22398
The modern Old Town Street runs more or less on the path of the old one. The spot where the carriage is driving is now on the pavement to the west of the Roundabout at St Andrew's Cross and on the south side of Royal Parade.

**BEDFORD STREET 1904** 52407

The imposing Prudential Building (centre) was damaged during the war, but still stood in 1945.
It was demolished in 1947 to make way for the new street plan. Its tower occupied a position which
today is on the west side of Armada Way near where the Western Morning News office now stands.

**BEDFORD STREET 1913** 65976
This scene shows some well-known Plymouth business-
es. Dingles (far left) are still in the town, although
these days owned by House of Fraser, and
Underwoods were well-known grocers. John Yeo, along
with Spooners (out of sight at the end of the street)
was eventually taken over by Debenhams.

**THE GUILDHALL AND BEDFORD STREET 1904** 52409

The Bedford Hotel later became Bateman's Opticians, with a giant pair of spectacles that many local people still remember. The northern end of the Post Office (just visible down Basket Street in the centre) would now be on Royal Parade outside Dingles.

**BEDFORD STREET 1913** 65975

Here we see more well-known Plymouth names. Many Plymothians remember buying school bags and suitcases from Webb and Son, who dealt in leather goods. Goodbody's Café was a popular spot, and indeed there is still a pub of that name on Mutley Plain.

**OLD TOWN STREET c1960** P60085

After the war, the remains of the city centre were demolished to make way for a new, more regular street plan. In this picture the new Post Office is still under construction on the right.

**ROYAL PARADE c1960** P60101

This photograph was taken from roughly the site of the old Post Office. The bus on the other side of Royal Parade behind the scooter is one of the first to have the door at the front and no conductor.

**DRAKE'S CIRCUS c1955** P60032

### DRAKE'S CIRCUS c1955
The Guinness clock at the top of Old Town Street was a popular rendezvous. It stood where the southern end of Drake's Circus shopping centre now stands. The corner this side of the obvious awnings is now home to Burton's.

◆

### COBOURG STREET c1955
The north side of Cobourg Street is almost unchanged. The Public Secondary School (right), whose most well-known old girl is Angela Rippon, is now part of the University of Plymouth, and the playground is occupied by satellite dishes.

**COBOURG STREET c1955** P60038

**POUND STREET c1955**  P60051

To the right of the junction at the far end of Pound Street is the Harvest Home, a much-loved pub which was demolished in 1964. The tall building beyond the Harvest Home still stands; it is home to hairdressers Maison Terry and a number of cafés.

**THE MUSEUM AND FREE LIBRARY 1892**  30581A

Although bombed during the war, the museum, art gallery and library are still at the bottom of Tavistock Road. Just out of the picture on the left was the surgery of the school dentist - something pointed out by almost every Plymothian over fifty to see this picture!

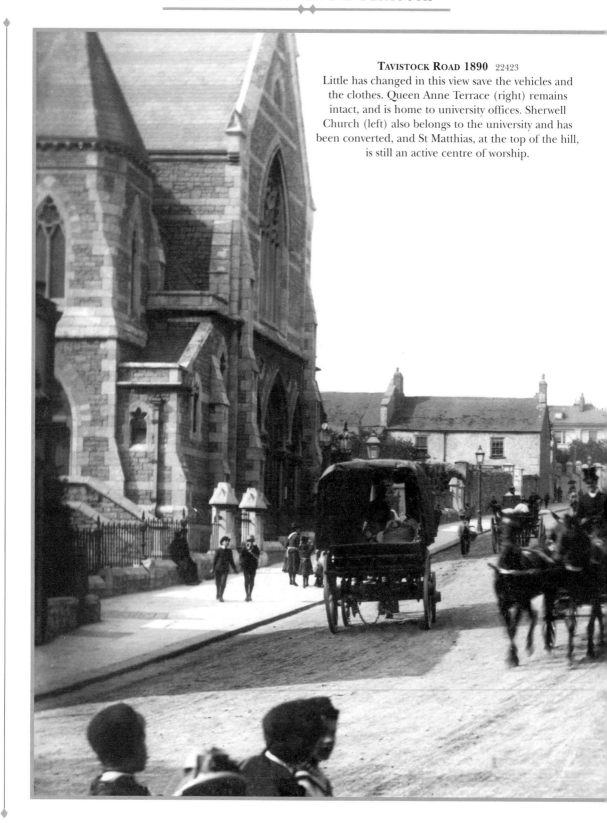

**TAVISTOCK ROAD 1890** 22423
Little has changed in this view save the vehicles and the clothes. Queen Anne Terrace (right) remains intact, and is home to university offices. Sherwell Church (left) also belongs to the university and has been converted, and St Matthias, at the top of the hill, is still an active centre of worship.

**MUTLEY PLAIN 1904** 52412
The private houses on the left are now occupied by pizza take-aways and newsagents. The Co-op is still on the same premises, albeit with a new frontage, and Mutley Baptist Church (left) remains unchanged. The house on the corner of Alexandra Road (right) was for many years a dentist's.

**MUTLEY PLAIN 1904** 52413
Take away the trees, update the shop frontages and turn the road into a dual carriageway, and you see Mutley as it is today, except that the Hyde Park Hotel (from where this view was taken) is now on an island and Mutley Methodist (left) has been pulled down.

**THE CATHOLIC CATHEDRAL 1889**
The Cathedral Church of St Margaret Mary, with its elegant slim spire, was started in 1856 by Bishop Vaughan. Next to it in this picture stands Notre Dame High School, run by nuns who lived in the convent attached to the school. The site is now occupied by sheltered housing.

**GEORGE STREET 1889**
The imposing columns are the entrance to the Theatre Royal, which stood on the site now occupied by the ABC Cinema. Theatregoers used to be able to hire a boy from the Barbican to queue for them, a service which cost the princely sum of 6d in the 1930s.

**THE CATHOLIC CATHEDRAL 1889** 22409

**GEORGE STREET 1889** 22397

**THE CLOCK TOWER 1892** 30597
Cousins' Hotel (left) and Genoni's, next to it, were
popular refreshment stops for actors and stage crew
between rehearsals. That function for the modern
Theatre Royal (built roughly on the site of the GWR
offices) is fulfilled by The Bank, which in this picture
(behind the columns) is still a bank.

**THE THEATRE ROYAL AND DERRY'S CLOCK 1907** 59204
Derry's Clock, erected in 1862 by Samuel Derry, was known to generations of Plymothians as 'the four-faced deceiver' because all the clock faces told slightly different times. The clock still stands behind the new Theatre Royal.

**THE CLOCK TOWER 1924** 75922

Derry's Clock had four drinking fountains at its base with cups (long since gone) that hung on chains. The underground toilets on the right reputedly had their 'Ladies' and 'Gents' signs swapped round by Lawrence of Arabia when he was stationed in Plymouth.

**UNION STREET 1889** 22359

A surprising amount of this part of Union Street still exists. The corner on the left is now taxi offices and the adjoining buildings are night clubs and shops. The projecting building at centre left is the Clipper pub. The Octagon (centre) was in 1890 private homes rather than burger, pizza and kebab houses.

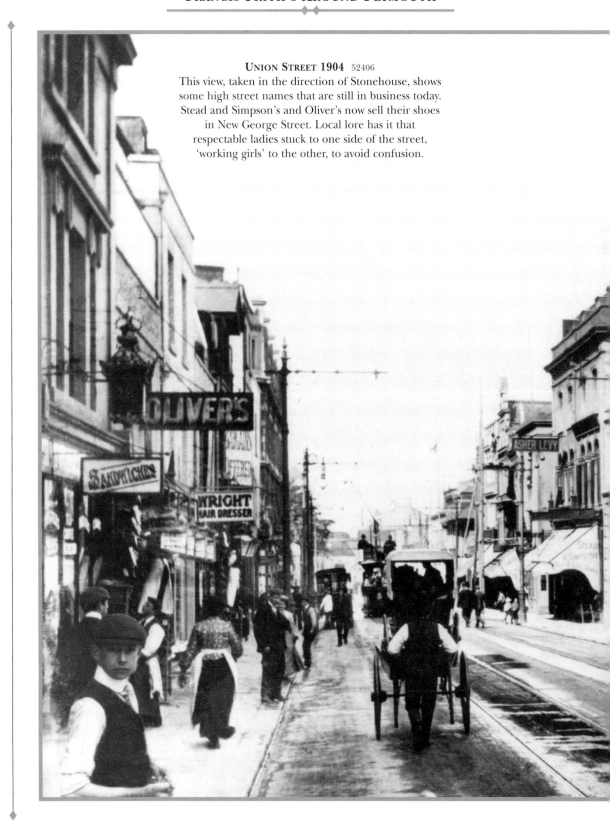

**UNION STREET 1904** 52406
This view, taken in the direction of Stonehouse, shows
some high street names that are still in business today.
Stead and Simpson's and Oliver's now sell their shoes
in New George Street. Local lore has it that
respectable ladies stuck to one side of the street,
'working girls' to the other, to avoid confusion.

**DEVONPORT, HALFPENNY BRIDGE 1904** 52427
Upstream of Halfpenny Bridge, Stonehouse creek used to run as far as Pennycomequick, but was progressively filled over the years. Downstream (right) from the bridge is the Cremyll Ferry and Royal Willam Yard. The toll-house was the white building on the left; the toll, as the name suggested, was a halfpenny.

**DEVONPORT, ROYAL MARINE BARRACKS 1890** 22448
Situated on Durnford Street, which runs parallel to Stonehouse Creek, the Royal Marine Barracks were built in 1867 using a mixture of Plymouth limestone and granite from the moors and originally housed 1400 men.

**DEVONPORT, MOUNT WISE 1890** 22468
A large marina now stands (or rather floats) on this site. The hill on the right has a memorial to Devonport's most famous son, Captain Scott, and on the riverside in the middle distance the large barn-like building is King Billy Yard, the oldest covered shipyard still standing in Europe.

DEVONPORT, BOER GUN 1904  52415A

## DEVONPORT
### *Boer Gun 1904*

Inscribed 'Ready Aye Ready', this captured Boer gun is a memorial to Royal Marines and sailors from HMS 'Doris'. Fittingly, it stands high on a hill overlooking the dockyard from which HMS 'Doris' would have sailed to South Africa.

## DEVONPORT
### *HMS 'Lion' and 'Implacable' 1890*

These old ships of the line were probably used as training ships for young recruits. Outdated, mothballed or paid-off vessels were often moored at this spot off the mouth of Millbrook Lake. The much-loved aircraft carrier 'Ark Royal' spent some years here prior to being towed away for scrap in 1979.

DEVONPORT, HMS 'LION' AND 'IMPLACABLE' 1890  22467

**DEVONPORT, TORPOINT FERRY BRIDGE 1890** 22462

Ferries crossed at this point since the 18th century, carrying not only people, carriages and goods but, from 1800, the post for the Truro coach. 'Jemima', built at Stonehouse, became the first steam ferry in service in 1826, but was quickly replaced by steam driven chain ferries.

**TORPOINT, THE FERRY 1925** 78415

The earliest ferries were little more than two hulls with a platform suspended between them, and the crossing could take some time owing to the strong tides that run in the Tamar. Modern chain ferries, little affected by the tides, rattle and clank their way across in about ten minutes.

**TORPOINT, THE FERRY c1955** T63003
The lorry at the head of the ferry queue is probably taking empties back to the Plymouth Brewery near Halfpenny Bridge in Stonehouse. Fondly remembered by older drinkers, Plymouth Brewery was eventually taken over by Courage; after that, the beer never tasted quite the same.

### TORPOINT
### *The Ferry c1955*

The steep loading ramp of the ferries caused problems for longer vehicles, which were in danger of grounding. The brown and cream Co-op coaches had a bevel taken off the rear bodywork to prevent this happening.

### TORPOINT
### *The Ferry c1955*

At one time cars were fitted so tightly onto the ferries that it was impossible to open the doors. The obvious dangers of this in case of fire or sinking caused a public outcry, and eventually the ferries were widened.

**TORPOINT, THE FERRY c1955** T63004

**TORPOINT, THE FERRY c1955** T63006

**TORPOINT, FORE STREET C1955** T63014

On the left is Wheeler's Hotel, and at the top of the street, just visible, is the hop leaf symbol of Simond's Brewery - once a common sight on local pubs. On the right are two trade names that are rarely seen today - Woodbines and Capstan Full Strength.

**TORPOINT, FORE STREET AND FERRY QUEUE C1955** T63015

The ferry queue no longer blocks Fore Street - it takes the road on the right down to a large waiting area by the river. The three men in white hats are probably 'Tiffies' - Artificers from the training establishment at HMS 'Fisgard', now closed.

SALTASH, ROYAL ALBERT BRIDGE 1890 22477
The rich fields of the Tamar Valley have long been the source of Plymouth's fruit and vegetables. Tamar barges such as the one in the centre of this picture would bring produce down from Calstock, Gunnislake and Bere Alston and land them at Cornwall Street in Devonport.

SALTASH, THE ROYAL ALBERT BRIDGE 1890 22480
The Royal Albert Bridge, completed in 1859, is a fitting memorial to the great Victorian engineer Isambard Kingdom Brunel. The Admiralty stipulated that it must be at least 100 feet above the water to allow the passage of ships.

**SALTASH, THE FERRY 1924** 76023

The earliest record of a ferry here dates from 1337. In 1832 a consortium led by the Earl of Morley established the first steam ferry. The vessel in this picture came to a sad end - it was sunk off Portreath while being towed to Wales after being sold.

**SALTASH, THE TAMAR BRIDGE C1965** S50091

The completion of the road bridge in 1961 signalled the end of the Saltash Ferry. The bridge and the Torpoint Ferry are managed by a joint committee, with revenues from the bridge subsidising the maintenance and running of the ferry.

**PLYMPTON, ST MARY'S 1890** 22512

On the right of the photograph in front of the church is the old priory. The monks had their own path through the woods to the church, where they had their own pews. Behind the church, hidden in the trees, is Plympton station, which closed in 1959, and in the centre of the picture is the old St Mary's Church of England School.

**PLYMPTON, THE TOWN HALL 1890** 22515

This view remains almost unchanged, save that the horse and cart have been replaced by the motor car. The arched walk under the Town Hall is known as the Butterwalk.

**PLYMPTON, RIDGEWAY 1898** 41943
Matthews' Bun Shop (right) was so famous for its hot
cross buns that people would walk for miles, even
from Plymouth, to sample its wares. There were often
long queues at 4.00am!

**PLYMOUTH, FERRY HOUSE AND PLANTATIONS 1901** 46333
The quiet estuary of the River Yealm (pronounced 'Yam') lies to the east of Plymouth. The foot ferry still runs at this spot, summoned by shouting 'over' or by whistling. The villages of Newton Ferrers and Noss Mayo lie just up the river to the left.

**BERE FERRERS 1898** 42257
Bere Ferrers lies north of Plymouth on the isolated peninsula that divides the estuaries of the Tamar and its tributary the Tavy (right). Bere Ferrers is the first stop on the Tamar Valley railway line which runs up to Gunnislake; it has the distinction of being one of the few lines on which the train sometimes stops to allow passengers to take photographs!

**PLYMOUTH, DRAKE'S ISLAND 1890** 22426
Now in Cornwall, Mount Edgecumbe, from where this picture was taken, was once part of Devon. The nearby village of Kingsand still has a stone showing where the boundary used to lie. The folly was constructed using stone from the tower of St Lawrence's church, which used to stand on the site now occupied by Royal William Yard in Stonehouse.

**PLYMOUTH, DRAKE'S ISLAND FROM MOUNT EDGECUMBE 1890** 22427
The broad channel between Drake's Island and Mount Edgecumbe, known as The Bridges, is only navigable via one narrow channel, which is why ships always appear to take 'the long way round', following Drake Passage to the east and north of the Island, as the three-master in this picture is probably doing.

**PLYMOUTH, FROM MOUNT EDGECUMBE 1890** 22425
In the centre is the Edgecumbes' Winter Villa, which later became the convent and nursing home Nazareth House. It was completely rebuilt after a fire. The grassy area to the left is Devil's Point, a popular picnic and walking spot.

**PLYMOUTH, MOUNT EDGECUMBE HOUSE 1890** 22436
The building of Mount Edgecumbe House was started by Piers Edgecumbe in 1539 and remodelled in the 17th and 18th centuries. It was badly damaged by German incendiaries in March 1941 and subsequently restored, but the highest tower in this picture was never rebuilt.

# Index

# Frith Book Co Titles

## www.francisfrith.co.uk

The Frith Book Company publishes over 100 new titles each year. A selection of those currently available are listed below. For latest catalogue please contact Frith Book Co.

Town Books 96 pages, approx 100 photos. County and Themed Books 128 pages, approx 150 photos (unless specified). All titles hardback laminated case and jacket except those indicated pb (paperback)

| Title | ISBN | Price | | Title | ISBN | Price |
|---|---|---|---|---|---|---|
| Amersham, Chesham & Rickmansworth (pb) | | | | Derby (pb) | 1-85937-367-4 | £9.99 |
| | 1-85937-340-2 | £9.99 | | Derbyshire (pb) | 1-85937-196-5 | £9.99 |
| Ancient Monuments & Stone Circles | 1-85937-143-4 | £17.99 | | Devon (pb) | 1-85937-297-x | £9.99 |
| Aylesbury (pb) | 1-85937-227-9 | £9.99 | | Dorset (pb) | 1-85937-269-4 | £9.99 |
| Bakewell | 1-85937-113-2 | £12.99 | | Dorset Churches | 1-85937-172-8 | £17.99 |
| Barnstaple (pb) | 1-85937-300-3 | £9.99 | | Dorset Coast (pb) | 1-85937-299-6 | £9.99 |
| Bath (pb) | 1-85937-419-0 | £9.99 | | Dorset Living Memories | 1-85937-210-4 | £14.99 |
| Bedford (pb) | 1-85937-205-8 | £9.99 | | Down the Severn | 1-85937-118-3 | £14.99 |
| Berkshire (pb) | 1-85937-191-4 | £9.99 | | Down the Thames (pb) | 1-85937-278-3 | £9.99 |
| Berkshire Churches | 1-85937-170-1 | £17.99 | | Down the Trent | 1-85937-311-9 | £14.99 |
| Blackpool (pb) | 1-85937-382-8 | £9.99 | | Dublin (pb) | 1-85937-231-7 | £9.99 |
| Bognor Regis (pb) | 1-85937-431-x | £9.99 | | East Anglia (pb) | 1-85937-265-1 | £9.99 |
| Bournemouth | 1-85937-067-5 | £12.99 | | East London | 1-85937-080-2 | £14.99 |
| Bradford (pb) | 1-85937-204-x | £9.99 | | East Sussex | 1-85937-130-2 | £14.99 |
| Brighton & Hove(pb) | 1-85937-192-2 | £8.99 | | Eastbourne | 1-85937-061-6 | £12.99 |
| Bristol (pb) | 1-85937-264-3 | £9.99 | | Edinburgh (pb) | 1-85937-193-0 | £8.99 |
| British Life A Century Ago (pb) | 1-85937-213-9 | £9.99 | | England in the 1880s | 1-85937-331-3 | £17.99 |
| Buckinghamshire (pb) | 1-85937-200-7 | £9.99 | | English Castles (pb) | 1-85937-434-4 | £9.99 |
| Camberley (pb) | 1-85937-222-8 | £9.99 | | English Country Houses | 1-85937-161-2 | £17.99 |
| Cambridge (pb) | 1-85937-422-0 | £9.99 | | Essex (pb) | 1-85937-270-8 | £9.99 |
| Cambridgeshire (pb) | 1-85937-420-4 | £9.99 | | Exeter | 1-85937-126-4 | £12.99 |
| Canals & Waterways (pb) | 1-85937-291-0 | £9.99 | | Exmoor | 1-85937-132-9 | £14.99 |
| Canterbury Cathedral (pb) | 1-85937-179-5 | £9.99 | | Falmouth | 1-85937-066-7 | £12.99 |
| Cardiff (pb) | 1-85937-093-4 | £9.99 | | Folkestone (pb) | 1-85937-124-8 | £9.99 |
| Carmarthenshire | 1-85937-216-3 | £14.99 | | Glasgow (pb) | 1-85937-190-6 | £9.99 |
| Chelmsford (pb) | 1-85937-310-0 | £9.99 | | Gloucestershire | 1-85937-102-7 | £14.99 |
| Cheltenham (pb) | 1-85937-095-0 | £9.99 | | Great Yarmouth (pb) | 1-85937-426-3 | £9.99 |
| Cheshire (pb) | 1-85937-271-6 | £9.99 | | Greater Manchester (pb) | 1-85937-266-x | £9.99 |
| Chester | 1-85937-090-x | £12.99 | | Guildford (pb) | 1-85937-410-7 | £9.99 |
| Chesterfield | 1-85937-378-x | £9.99 | | Hampshire (pb) | 1-85937-279-1 | £9.99 |
| Chichester (pb) | 1-85937-228-7 | £9.99 | | Hampshire Churches (pb) | 1-85937-207-4 | £9.99 |
| Colchester (pb) | 1-85937-188-4 | £8.99 | | Harrogate | 1-85937-423-9 | £9.99 |
| Cornish Coast | 1-85937-163-9 | £14.99 | | Hastings & Bexhill (pb) | 1-85937-131-0 | £9.99 |
| Cornwall (pb) | 1-85937-229-5 | £9.99 | | Heart of Lancashire (pb) | 1-85937-197-3 | £9.99 |
| Cornwall Living Memories | 1-85937-248-1 | £14.99 | | Helston (pb) | 1-85937-214-7 | £9.99 |
| Cotswolds (pb) | 1-85937-230-9 | £9.99 | | Hereford (pb) | 1-85937-175-2 | £9.99 |
| Cotswolds Living Memories | 1-85937-255-4 | £14.99 | | Herefordshire | 1-85937-174-4 | £14.99 |
| County Durham | 1-85937-123-x | £14.99 | | Hertfordshire (pb) | 1-85937-247-3 | £9.99 |
| Croydon Living Memories | 1-85937-162-0 | £9.99 | | Horsham (pb) | 1-85937-432-8 | £9.99 |
| Cumbria | 1-85937-101-9 | £14.99 | | Humberside | 1-85937-215-5 | £14.99 |
| Dartmoor | 1-85937-145-0 | £14.99 | | Hythe, Romney Marsh & Ashford | 1-85937-256-2 | £9.99 |

# Available from your local bookshop or from the publisher

# Frith Book Co Titles (continued)

| | | | | | |
|---|---|---|---|---|---|
| Ipswich (pb) | 1-85937-424-7 | £9.99 | St Ives (pb) | 1-85937415-8 | £9.99 |
| Ireland (pb) | 1-85937-181-7 | £9.99 | Scotland (pb) | 1-85937-182-5 | £9.99 |
| Isle of Man (pb) | 1-85937-268-6 | £9.99 | Scottish Castles (pb) | 1-85937-323-2 | £9.99 |
| Isles of Scilly | 1-85937-136-1 | £14.99 | Sevenoaks & Tunbridge | 1-85937-057-8 | £12.99 |
| Isle of Wight (pb) | 1-85937-429-8 | £9.99 | Sheffield, South Yorks (pb) | 1-85937-267-8 | £9.99 |
| Isle of Wight Living Memories | 1-85937-304-6 | £14.99 | Shrewsbury (pb) | 1-85937-325-9 | £9.99 |
| Kent (pb) | 1-85937-189-2 | £9.99 | Shropshire (pb) | 1-85937-326-7 | £9.99 |
| Kent Living Memories | 1-85937-125-6 | £14.99 | Somerset | 1-85937-153-1 | £14.99 |
| Lake District (pb) | 1-85937-275-9 | £9.99 | South Devon Coast | 1-85937-107-8 | £14.99 |
| Lancaster, Morecambe & Heysham (pb) | 1-85937-233-3 | £9.99 | South Devon Living Memories | 1-85937-168-x | £14.99 |
| Leeds (pb) | 1-85937-202-3 | £9.99 | South Hams | 1-85937-220-1 | £14.99 |
| Leicester | 1-85937-073-x | £12.99 | Southampton (pb) | 1-85937-427-1 | £9.99 |
| Leicestershire (pb) | 1-85937-185-x | £9.99 | Southport (pb) | 1-85937-425-5 | £9.99 |
| Lincolnshire (pb) | 1-85937-433-6 | £9.99 | Staffordshire | 1-85937-047-0 | £12.99 |
| Liverpool & Merseyside (pb) | 1-85937-234-1 | £9.99 | Stratford upon Avon | 1-85937-098-5 | £12.99 |
| London (pb) | 1-85937-183-3 | £9.99 | Suffolk (pb) | 1-85937-221-x | £9.99 |
| Ludlow (pb) | 1-85937-176-0 | £9.99 | Suffolk Coast | 1-85937-259-7 | £14.99 |
| Luton (pb) | 1-85937-235-x | £9.99 | Surrey (pb) | 1-85937-240-6 | £9.99 |
| Maidstone | 1-85937-056-x | £14.99 | Sussex (pb) | 1-85937-184-1 | £9.99 |
| Manchester (pb) | 1-85937-198-1 | £9.99 | Swansea (pb) | 1-85937-167-1 | £9.99 |
| Middlesex | 1-85937-158-2 | £14.99 | Tees Valley & Cleveland | 1-85937-211-2 | £14.99 |
| New Forest | 1-85937-128-0 | £14.99 | Thanet (pb) | 1-85937-116-7 | £9.99 |
| Newark (pb) | 1-85937-366-6 | £9.99 | Tiverton (pb) | 1-85937-178-7 | £9.99 |
| Newport, Wales (pb) | 1-85937-258-9 | £9.99 | Torbay | 1-85937-063-2 | £12.99 |
| Newquay (pb) | 1-85937-421-2 | £9.99 | Truro | 1-85937-147-7 | £12.99 |
| Norfolk (pb) | 1-85937-195-7 | £9.99 | Victorian and Edwardian Cornwall | 1-85937-252-x | £14.99 |
| Norfolk Living Memories | 1-85937-217-1 | £14.99 | Victorian & Edwardian Devon | 1-85937-253-8 | £14.99 |
| Northamptonshire | 1-85937-150-7 | £14.99 | Victorian & Edwardian Kent | 1-85937-149-3 | £14.99 |
| Northumberland Tyne & Wear (pb) | 1-85937-281-3 | £9.99 | Vic & Ed Maritime Album | 1-85937-144-2 | £17.99 |
| North Devon Coast | 1-85937-146-9 | £14.99 | Victorian and Edwardian Sussex | 1-85937-157-4 | £14.99 |
| North Devon Living Memories | 1-85937-261-9 | £14.99 | Victorian & Edwardian Yorkshire | 1-85937-154-x | £14.99 |
| North London | 1-85937-206-6 | £14.99 | Victorian Seaside | 1-85937-159-0 | £17.99 |
| North Wales (pb) | 1-85937-298-8 | £9.99 | Villages of Devon (pb) | 1-85937-293-7 | £9.99 |
| North Yorkshire (pb) | 1-85937-236-8 | £9.99 | Villages of Kent (pb) | 1-85937-294-5 | £9.99 |
| Norwich (pb) | 1-85937-194-9 | £8.99 | Villages of Sussex (pb) | 1-85937-295-3 | £9.99 |
| Nottingham (pb) | 1-85937-324-0 | £9.99 | Warwickshire (pb) | 1-85937-203-1 | £9.99 |
| Nottinghamshire (pb) | 1-85937-187-6 | £9.99 | Welsh Castles (pb) | 1-85937-322-4 | £9.99 |
| Oxford (pb) | 1-85937-411-5 | £9.99 | West Midlands (pb) | 1-85937-289-9 | £9.99 |
| Oxfordshire (pb) | 1-85937-430-1 | £9.99 | West Sussex | 1-85937-148-5 | £14.99 |
| Peak District (pb) | 1-85937-280-5 | £9.99 | West Yorkshire (pb) | 1-85937-201-5 | £9.99 |
| Penzance | 1-85937-069-1 | £12.99 | Weymouth (pb) | 1-85937-209-0 | £9.99 |
| Peterborough (pb) | 1-85937-219-8 | £9.99 | Wiltshire (pb) | 1-85937-277-5 | £9.99 |
| Piers | 1-85937-237-6 | £17.99 | Wiltshire Churches (pb) | 1-85937-171-x | £9.99 |
| Plymouth | 1-85937-119-1 | £12.99 | Wiltshire Living Memories | 1-85937-245-7 | £14.99 |
| Poole & Sandbanks (pb) | 1-85937-251-1 | £9.99 | Winchester (pb) | 1-85937-428-x | £9.99 |
| Preston (pb) | 1-85937-212-0 | £9.99 | Windmills & Watermills | 1-85937-242-2 | £17.99 |
| Reading (pb) | 1-85937-238-4 | £9.99 | Worcester (pb) | 1-85937-165-5 | £9.99 |
| Romford (pb) | 1-85937-319-4 | £9.99 | Worcestershire | 1-85937-152-3 | £14.99 |
| Salisbury (pb) | 1-85937-239-2 | £9.99 | York (pb) | 1-85937-199-x | £9.99 |
| Scarborough (pb) | 1-85937-379-8 | £9.99 | Yorkshire (pb) | 1-85937-186-8 | £9.99 |
| St Albans (pb) | 1-85937-341-0 | £9.99 | Yorkshire Living Memories | 1-85937-166-3 | £14.99 |

## See Frith books on the internet www.francisfrith.co.uk

# FRITH PRODUCTS & SERVICES

Francis Frith would doubtless be pleased to know that the pioneering publishing venture he started in 1860 still continues today. A hundred and forty years later, The Francis Frith Collection continues in the same innovative tradition and is now one of the foremost publishers of vintage photographs in the world. Some of the current activities include:

## Interior Decoration

Today Frith's photographs can be seen framed and as giant wall murals in thousands of pubs, restaurants, hotels, banks, retail stores and other public buildings throughout the country. In every case they enhance the unique local atmosphere of the places they depict and provide reminders of gentler days in an increasingly busy and frenetic world.

## Product Promotions

Frith products are used by many major companies to promote the sales of their own products or to reinforce their own history and heritage. Frith promotions have been used by Hovis bread, Courage beers, Scots Porage Oats, Colman's mustard, Cadbury's foods, Mellow Birds coffee, Dunhill pipe tobacco, Guinness, and Bulmer's Cider.

## Genealogy and Family History

As the interest in family history and roots grows world-wide, more and more people are turning to Frith's photographs of Great Britain for images of the towns, villages and streets where their ancestors lived; and, of course, photographs of the churches and chapels where their ancestors were christened, married and buried are an essential part of every genealogy tree and family album.

## Frith Products

All Frith photographs are available Framed or just as Mounted Prints and Posters (size 23 x 16 inches). These may be ordered from the address below. From time to time other products - Address Books, Calendars, Table Mats, etc - are available.

## The Internet

Already twenty thousand Frith photographs can be viewed and purchased on the internet through the Frith websites and a myriad of partner sites.

For more detailed information on Frith companies and products, look at these sites:

www.francisfrith.co.uk
www.francisfrith.com
*(for North American visitors)*

---

**See the complete list of Frith Books at:**

*www.francisfrith.co.uk*

This web site is regularly updated with the latest list of publications from the Frith Book Company. If you wish to buy books relating to another part of the country that your local bookshop does not stock, you may purchase on-line.

---

*For further information, trade, or author enquiries please contact us at the address below:*
**The Francis Frith Collection, Frith's Barn, Teffont, Salisbury, Wiltshire, England SP3 5QP.**
Tel: +44 (0)1722 716 376  Fax: +44 (0)1722 716 881   Email: sales@francisfrith.co.uk

# See Frith books on the internet www.francisfrith.co.uk

# TO RECEIVE YOUR **FREE** MOUNTED PRINT

**Mounted Print**
*Overall size 14 x 11 inches*

*Cut out this Voucher and return it with your remittance for £1.95 to cover postage and handling, to UK addresses. For overseas addresses please include £4.00 post and handling. Choose any photograph included in this book. Your SEPIA print will be A4 in size, and mounted in a cream mount with burgundy rule line, overall size 14 x 11 inches.*

## Order additional Mounted Prints at HALF PRICE (only £7.49 each*)

If there are further pictures you would like to order, possibly as gifts for friends and family, purchase them at half price (no additional postage and handling required).

## Have your Mounted Prints framed*

For an additional £14.95 per print you can have your chosen Mounted Print framed in an elegant polished wood and gilt moulding, overall size 16 x 13 inches (no additional postage and handling required).

---

**\* IMPORTANT!**
These special prices are only available if ordered using the original voucher on this page (no copies permitted) and at the same time as your free Mounted Print, for delivery to the same address

---

## Frith Collectors' Guild

*From time to time we publish a magazine of news and stories about Frith photographs and further special offers of Frith products. If you would like 12 months FREE membership, please return this form.*

---

*Send completed forms to:*
**The Francis Frith Collection, Frith's Barn, Teffont, Salisbury, Wiltshire SP3 5QP**

---

# *Voucher* for **FREE** and Reduced Price Frith Prints

| Picture no. | Page number | Qty | Mounted @ £7.49 | Framed + £14.95 | Total Cost |
|---|---|---|---|---|---|
| | | 1 | **Free of charge\*** | £ | £ |
| | | | £7.49 | £ | £ |
| | | | £7.49 | £ | £ |
| | | | £7.49 | £ | £ |
| | | | £7.49 | £ | £ |
| | | | £7.49 | £ | £ |

| | | |
|---|---|---|
| *Please allow 28 days for delivery* | **\* Post & handling** | **£1.95** |
| **Book Title** . . . . . . . . . . . . . . . | **Total Order Cost** | **£** |

***Please do not photocopy this voucher. Only the original is valid, so please cut it out and return it to us.***

I enclose a cheque / postal order for £ . . . . . . . . . .
made payable to 'The Francis Frith Collection'
OR please debit my Mastercard / Visa / Switch / Amex card
*(credit cards please on all overseas orders)*

Number . . . . . . . . . . . . . . . . . . . . . . . . . . . . . . . .

Issue No(Switch only) . . . . . . . .Valid from (Amex/Switch) . . . . . . .

Expires . . . . . . . . . . Signature . . . . . . . . . . . . . . . .

Name  Mr/Mrs/Ms . . . . . . . . . . . . . . . . . . . . . . . . . . . . .

Address . . . . . . . . . . . . . . . . . . . . . . . . . . . . . . . . . .

. . . . . . . . . . . . . . . . . . . . . . . . . . . . . . . . . . . . . . . .

. . . . . . . . . . . . . . . . . . . . . . . . Postcode . . . . . . . . . . . .

Daytime Tel No . . . . . . . . . . . . . . . . . . . . . .    Valid to 31/12/02

---

# The Francis Frith Collectors' Guild

Please enrol me as a member for 12 months free of charge.

Name  Mr/Mrs/Ms . . . . . . . . . . . . . . . . . . . . . . . . . . . . .

Address . . . . . . . . . . . . . . . . . . . . . . . . . . . . . . . . . .

. . . . . . . . . . . . . . . . . . . . . . . . . . . . . . . . . . . . . . . .

. . . . . . . . . . . . . . . . . . . . . . . . Postcode . . . . . . . . . . . .

**Would you like to find out more about Francis Frith?**

We have recently recruited some entertaining speakers who are happy to visit local groups, clubs and societies to give an illustrated talk documenting Frith's travels and photographs. If you are a member of such a group and are interested in hosting a presentation, we would love to hear from you.

Our speakers bring with them a small selection of our local town and county books, together with sample prints. They are happy to take orders. A small proportion of the order value is donated to the group who have hosted the presentation. The talks are therefore an excellent way of fundraising for small groups and societies.

**Can you help us with information about any of the Frith photographs in this book?**

We are gradually compiling an historical record for each of the photographs in the Frith archive. It is always fascinating to find out the names of the people shown in the pictures, as well as insights into the shops, buildings and other features depicted.

If you recognize anyone in the photographs in this book, or if you have information not already included in the author's caption, do let us know. We would love to hear from you, and will try to publish it in future books or articles.

**Our production team**

Frith books are produced by a small dedicated team at offices in the converted Grade II listed 18th-century barn at Teffont near Salisbury, illustrated above. Most have worked with the Frith Collection for many years. All have in common one quality: they have a passion for the Frith Collection. The team is constantly expanding, but currently includes:

Jason Buck, John Buck, Douglas Burns, Heather Crisp, Isobel Hall, Rob Hames, Hazel Heaton, Peter Horne, James Kinnear, Tina Leary, Hannah Marsh, Eliza Sackett, Terence Sackett, Sandra Sanger, Shelley Tolcher, Susanna Walker, Clive Wathen and Jenny Wathen.